Mother's M.

Mother's Milk

A SEQUENCE OF POEMS

W. G. SHEPHERD

MENARD PRESS
2006

Mother's Milk © W. G. Shepherd 2006

All rights reserved

ISBN 1 874320 56 X

Menard Press
8 The Oaks, Woodside Avenue, London N12 8AR, UK
Tel. + 44 (0)20 8446 5571   Fax + 44 (020) 8445 2990
Email: Menard@Menardpress.co.uk
www.menardpress.co.uk

Representation
Inpress Limited, Northumberland House
11 The Pavement, Popes Lane, Ealing, London W5 4NG
Tel: 020 8832 7464   Fax: 020 8832 7465
Email: stephanie@inpressbooks.co.uk
www.inpressbooks.co.uk

Worldwide Distribution (except North America)
Central Books (Troika), 99 Wallis Road
Hackney Wick, London E9 5LN
Tel: 020 8986 4854
www.centralbooks.com

Distribution in North America
Small Press Distribution Inc.
1341 Seventh Street, Berkeley, CA 94710, USA
www.spdbooks.org

For details of the epigraph copyright, see page 48

Typeset by Antony Gray
Printed in Great Britain by
Cambridge University Press

Contents

PART ONE

Blushful Hippocrene	13
Underfloor Heating	15
Puppet	15
The Growth Furnace	16
Sackcloth Seraglio	17
The Word	18
Gents Tanka	20
Out of My Pram	20
Fantastically Reasonable	21
The Hangover Dream	23
The Whisky Talking	25
Nth Attempt at Weaning	27
Verbal Corkscrew	28
Psychozenthesis	28

PART TWO

Fresh Start	31
Open	33
The Gift	34
Genesis	35
The Stormcock	36
Spiritus	38
Mortals	38
No	39
Remorse	40

The Beloved	41
Strindberg's 'Wave VII'	43
Come to Me	43
All is Well	44
The Pursuit of Happiness	45
Cranial Osteopathy	46
The Almond Tree Shall Flourish	47
Note	48

For Margaret,
My Loyal Shepherdess

His craving for alcohol was the equivalent on a low level of the spiritual thirst of our being for wholeness, expressed in medieval language: the union with God. 'As the hart panteth after the water brooks, so panteth my soul after thee, O God' (Psalm 42:1).

How could one formulate such an insight in a language that is not misunderstood in our days? . . .

. . . alcohol in Latin is *spiritus* and you use the same word for the highest religious experience. The helpful motto therefore is: *spiritus contra spiritum.*

from C. G. Jung's letter of 30 January 1961
to Bill Wilson, co-founder of
Alcoholics Anonymous

Part One

Blushful Hippocrene

When Zeus had got Semele with child
The girl, egged on by the jealous Hera,
Pestered the god to throw off
His assumed humanity and reveal
His true godhead. At last he consented –
A thunderous blast of lightning

Felled Semele. Zeus removed
From her dead womb the living embryo
And lodged it in his thigh
From which, in the course of nature,
The baby was duly born –
A boy, Dionysus, god of wine.

It was not canny to resist
The irresistible progress of Dionysus.
Lycurgus, king of Thrace, disapproved of the cult
And seized the god, who made him mad,
So that he killed his own son, thinking
He was hacking down a vine.

Pentheus, king of Thebes,
Refused to allow Dionysus to enter that city,
But the god persuaded the king to watch the orgies
And Pentheus was caught and dismembered
By the blind-drunk Theban women
Led by his own mother.

I have before me a bottle
Of Châteauneuf du Pape, 1977,
Opened, potent, fragrant, breathing,
And a tear-shaped litre
Of Perrier water, in misty condensation
Because it is chilled.

To look directly at a Gorgon,
The tangle of snakes erupting from her scalp
And her ravaged, searing features,
Even if she were dead,
Caused the observer to change
Instantly to solid stone.

When the hero Perseus
Who flew upon winged sandals
Beheaded the Gorgon Medusa
Her blood, as it splashed on the ground,
Transmuted instantly and leapt up
As the winged horse Pegasus.

When Pegasus alighted with a clap
Of his thunderous wings on Mount Helicon
He struck the ground with his hoof
And water sprang from the stone.
This was Hippocrene, the Muses' spring
Of inspiration, cold, pure, crystalline water.

Underfloor Heating

We roll back the carpet to dance
And find the floor is transparent glass.

Beneath it chops and swings
The fascinating hangman Lava,

The buried god. We crawl
Across his boiling face.

Puppet

The mad god Alcohol
Has shoved

His hand up my arse
And works me:

Hence my bloody
Jokes and threats.

The Growth Furnace

Thy heart a black cabbage in
Crystal, supernova.
And an ice age. And an ice age.

Through a silver diffuser
Into a reservoir containing arsenic chloride,
The first zone of the growth furnace.

Satanic virginals whence
Slavery and the death of thy spirit as a bad
Breath. Must be loved at a distance:

Close-to the light
Destroys like the love of God.
And slavery flows

Like a bad breath. Everyday objects –
Chair, waste-paper basket – surely they must
Explode in a whirlwind of flame.

Reality stands in the sky.
Ice, cramp, ephemera, carnation,
Blink.

Sackcloth Seraglio

Era in iron genera, needle
Point cause and effect, these chains:
Desuetude, raillery, hoyden.

Howling wilderness of
Silk, surgeons fête cuckoo, god, alike.
Chop chopper chops chorale.

Little hands plead, for seed
Is cause, is posterity. Skid, slab
And slay, dirty bungler, that sisterhood

In the closet, at the feast.
Soften, ringmaster, palliative pity
Soft-hearted, soggy.

Ah! modest immodesty postured out –
A thousand sequestered madonnas:
This is the pox and its generation.

The Word

Shavaster
Is the name of a planet,
Its people and their language. That language
Consists of only one word
Which is, of course, 'shavaster'.
The multitudinous meanings required are introduced
In the way the Shavaster say the word:
By this means Shavaster is made
As efficient and expressive a language
As English.

In order to speak and understand
Shavaster, the Shavaster
Are attuned exquisitely
To infinitesimal variations
In pitch, tempo, volume, duration,
Pronunciation, emphasis, timbre
And so forth. They are equally alive
To body language: someone's pupils dilate,
Their diameter increasing
By one thousandth of a millimetre:
This is perceived and understood.

Their supreme acuity
Of awareness has brought the Shavaster
To a state of God-like empathy: in love
For one another they swim
And drown. Most of them lose their reason
Or take their own lives
Because of the intolerable burden
Of experiencing constantly, in merciless fullness,
The joys and sorrows of all
With whom they converse.

       shavas tat savash
           savashta vastava
       shava sterashta va
           ta vasa vash

       shavast atsavash
           savash tavast ava
       shavaster ash tava
           tava savash

       shavasta tsavash
           savash tavastava
       shavast erashtava
           tavasav ash

The foregoing
Is the shavaster *Shavaster*, by Shavaster.
Its acknowledged greatness inheres
In the way its notation
For the word 'shavaster' (or rather
For an infinite number of versions
Of 'shavaster', depending on how the word is spoken)
Is placed among congruous notations
Approximating to notations for versions
Of 'shavaster'. The work implies
The creation or revelation,
The simultaneous imminence and presence,
Of no less than everything. The word
Is THE WORD.

What I have written here
Is itself, or would be
If read on Shavaster, an example
Of the art of shavaster – a 'found'
Shavaster, as it were. However,
My notation for 'shavaster' is not set
Congruously, as is Shavaster's,
But sprinkled at random upon sheer nonsense.
It is as though the universe were pluralised
Within a further universe
Which is chaos.

Gents Tanka

Drunk, I waste ninety
Seconds of life's brevity
Trying to persuade
The condom vending-machine
To blow hot air on my hands

Out of My Pram

I could climb out of my pram
If I would – but I won't. Not yet.
I'm trying to want to climb out.

I'm trying to give up milk.
I may drop my bottle over the side –
No mum is pushing my pram.

Fantastically Reasonable

1

I want you, personally, to care
About me, personally. Why do you not
Like me? It is not difficult.

If I don't feel, as a reality,
Not just deduce, that you care about me,
I cannot take you or myself

Entirely seriously. I want to hear
Criticism conforming to the template,
'It's all right, I still like you, but . . . '

I will tell you what's what
And you shall dispense, doctor, the placebo
Advice, the analgesic compassion.

2

I am what?
Unreasonable? Well now,
Let me give you

Some thousand reasons
To convince you that I am,
Precisely, reasonable.

I am
Fantastically reasonable,
Upon occasion.

Any occasion.
You provide the occasion
And I will reason.

3

If you try to tell me that I am less generous,
Less concerned, than I am accustomed to suppose,
I may fail to understand.

This is not wilful stupidity: it is quite genuine.
Your words are not in themselves difficult
And they fit together syntactically,

Yet you have suddenly become
Extremely obscure and allusive,
Or lapsed into Aztec. My blankness

Makes you in turn feel stupid.
You have failed to enable me
To understand. You fool.

The Hangover Dream

Depression seems inevitable,
But do I really have to enact it?
Am I a bona fide patient,
From the Latin *patior*, 'I suffer'?

The anxious man in the next bed
Greets me warmly, garrulously.
He and I seem very much alike.
In fact he is me. His claims are irksome.

Exiting through the window
Like Peter Pan, I fly about vaguely all night
In oblivious darkness,
Returning severely hung over.

My brother has undergone drastic surgery.
It is as though the doctor has used an axe.
A single blow has sliced from each hand
The first two fingers, the thumb

And a large part of the palm. Both legs
Are lopped at the knee.
The new surfaces created by these croppings
Are neat and flat, and painted pink.

The tongue remains, and functions.
With a reproachful-forgiving implication –
Because I have been absent for some time
And have not thought of him once –

He says confidently
That he really feels much better
And will soon be as well as me.
Plainly, he is dying.

Colic grips him.
He freezes in agony.
Two nurses try to help him to a bedpan.
Clotted blood squirts from his anus.

What rubbish. What poor stuff.
How tedious. Insulting. Well,
I am not much moved or interested.
I switch off and wake.

The Whisky Talking

1

Is ill?
Damned? Hurts
All right. Doesn't want
Remission.

Prays
Yet disbelieves –
Make-believe
Makes no belief.

Swims
In a womb, in slag. Hugs
Its fear. Drinks up
Its venom.

Knows
What's what. Can do
Whatever. Nothing
Is enough, is all.

2

Castrated, quadruply amputated,
Blinded, made deaf,

Stoppered and drip-fed,
Floating submerged in tepidity,

Totally sense-deprived
Yet the sensorium continually blasted,

Thoughts twittering and gibbering
Under torture being administered by no one,

Brain massive, rock-solid
And insupportably heavy, grey blood,

Active squirming again supplanting
A state so uninteresting it precludes comment,

Resurgence of life giving back hope
For sufficient will to die.

Nth Attempt at Weaning

I gather my treasure, my bottles,
And pour them out down the sink,
Shaking them, trying to make the liquor –
Tricksy milk from an absent breast –
Gush out faster. I clench my face
In a rictus beyond delight and agony
And I cry. Why such an extreme ecstasy?
Because I'm dying, because I'm being born,
Perhaps because I sense and deny
The impossible presence of God the Mother.

Verbal Corkscrew

Black pots dragging on fags tut-tut
At my drinking kettle. Liver or lungs, whatever,
We tease Death, we try to get Death going.

Psychozenthesis
for Maggie

'I must escape
From the wheel of drinking, thinking
And sleep . . .'

My counsellor grabs her stick –

'Escape? Where is he?
Show me the villain who binds you
Against your will!'

Part Two

Fresh Start

1

All the alcohol
Has drained now from my body
And, I think, spirit.
I begin to feel and know
That I do belong on Earth.

The silent screaming
In my brain has faded out.
I'm listening now
To quietness, the patient
Silence preceding music.

My life is simple.
I will to do, as always,
What I want to do.
I want now to do the will
Of the God whose love I seek.

2

I had forgotten
The cool sun, the peaceful face
Of my own spirit.
He is the presence of God
In me, my own face aged two.

I pray to catch sight
Of that cheerfulness again,
Live, in a mirror.

I work now for him,
For the pleasure of being sane,
For sobriety.
It is repetitive work
But I enjoy the sunshine.

My grown-up knowledge
Desires to dare quietly
To meet my own eyes.

Open

Uncreated beings live on bliss,
Bliss is their food. They create themselves
By eating earth here on Earth.

> *– after a Pali myth*

    There's enough clearance
    In all my joints:

    My skull's not welded
    To my backbone:

    My chest holds generous room
    For lungs and heart:

    My shoulders want to open
    Like a fan, to unfold into wings –

    I have an angel inside me. He and I
    Imagine and so enact

    A blossoming out. A spring wells up
    In a cool boiling

    And flows outward
    In a chosen heartfelt letting go.

    I touch my fingers to my breastbone
    Then open my arms wide

    Offering my embrace
    To someone higher than myself –

    I tilt back my head
    Eyes open   and am   open.

The Gift

Ego:

Today the sunshine
Is like being loved strenuously
From the sky. Bright darkness

Hangs intricately
Beneath the blackbird's prunus tree.
Written on silence and light

Eternity seems now.
Come forward into my senses. I offer
This garden reality to you.

Angel:

Chocolate crimson
The bunches of foliage! And liquid
Muscular warblings!

Thank you, my love. I relish
Such gifts of human being.
And in the dimension of time

I am with you
Until our wave lapses
Back into ocean.

Genesis

1

The blackbird is a small dinosaur
Descended by way of the archaeopteryx:

No wonder his signature
Is so distilled, so delicious –

The godhead has been practising him
For a long time.

2

The universe
Is the uncreated God trying
To create himself

And the blackbird's song,
Like intelligence, or kindness,
Is an instance of grace

Getting through
From the uncreated realm
Into this reality.

3

This enraptured virtuosity
In a *raga* for a sunny morning,

This spontaneous outcry learned by rote
Down a million years,

Is in the hearing so sensual
That it is spiritual.

The Stormcock

Crying *What I do is me: for that I came.*
— GERARD MANLEY HOPKINS

From behind the church
A huge invasion
Of indigo wet-slate blackness
Surges up slowly
Quenching the sky.

A missel-thrush
Flies across the gardens
And perches on the topmost twig
Of our thirty foot ash tree
To sing at the storm.

The evening sun
Lights him horizontally
In golden detail.

The thrush's utterance –
Liquid, repetitive, engrossed, torrential, loud –
Induces in my chest a delight
As though my heart were being stroked
By an angel. And his dew-wet
Clarity of timbre pulls gently
At etheric muscles
In my throat and mouth.

Perhaps he smells rain, foretells
Emergence of earthworms. I watch
The opening and closing
Of his bill, the violent fluttering
Of his throat and the heaving
Of his bellows breast – he is all
Music, statement, assertion.

When the sun is muffled
By the storm's advance
The thrush flies away
To attend to other matters.

Spiritus

I snuffle ordinary air
Freshened by rain, clarified by sun
And charged with molecules

From the hawthorn seething with may
And I know, I know by my reverent joy
In that nourishing erotic reek

I'm a child of God, my nose
Connected to my soul, each chestful
Of spirit brightening the blood.

Mortals

Look at me! – I'm an old man
Riding the dragon as a novice surfer
Rides a wave – a tidal wave.

Mother, your molten rock heart must cool,
Your glistening blue and white sheath of life
Must finally be extinguished. Meanwhile

I'm more or less contentedly
Riding bareback your unbroken dragon
Whose love is 'Live. Now die.'

No

I include, as always,
An inconsolably weeping baby
Called Hunger. His face
Is congested with rage and grief.
His little perfect mouth
Frames a rectangular yell.
His protest is intertwined
With my will to live,
And yet is unbearably hopeless.

I could pacify Hunger,
Silence his dreadful outcry
With the drug I taught him to crave –
But I meet my Angel in this commandment
Clear and sharp-edged
As a beam of white light in dark mist:
'You   shall   *not!*' –
And in this prohibition
I know the balm of being loved.

Hunger's tear-drowned glare
Of reproach and indignation
Does not seek our long-dead mother
But demands relief of *me* –
His eyes meet mine: I
Am our mother and father now.
My heart feels heavy with love
And one of my loving words
Is 'No!'

Remorse

My victims, please come
Into the light.

I feel you enter
My hands. A paralysis

Creeps up my arms –
I fear for my heart.

Wisdom stomachs
This blackish savour.

The Beloved

> Common as light is love,
> And its familiar voice wearies not ever;
> Like the wide heaven, the all-sustaining air,
> It makes the reptile equal to the God . . .
>   – *Prometheus Unbound*, II, V

Being created into the light
First comes the odalisque
Piercingly lovely, in love with herself
Deliciously dancing
In her little silk knickers
And a choker of pearls. She is like a keyhole
For which there is no key
Through whom might sometimes be glimpsed
The uncreated Beloved.

Second comes her lustful suitor
Singing ecstatic arias
In a virile, passionate soprano voice.
He is like a bird of paradise
And a missel-thrush singing at the storm.
He is a Baroque castrato
Impotent till death.

Third comes the eunuch's brother
The raving drunk
Cirrhotic and toothless
Senile at forty. Listen carefully:
His deranged mouthings
Are a language of great precision and clarity –
He defines exactly
The quality and depth of his rage.

The ravenous baby
With the yelling rectangular mouth
Falls silent and gazes
In tear-blurred fascination . . .
The two-year-old Buddha-cum-Narcissus
Shifts his bottom in the shallow rock-pool
To turn and watch with benign serenity . . .

Baby and little boy by looking
Distil from the three a fourth comer.
Who is she? Where? I can't see her.

She is like foliage in spring sunshine
Through which light passes. I have glimpsed
In the depths of my mirrored face
Her translucent image against the light.
By being illumined, by being steeped in light
The leaf makes light visible.

Strindberg's 'Wave VII'

As it rolls forward out of the painting
Beneath a sky of agglomerated slabs
Of grey darkness and sparse white light

I would take a header into the face
Of that mighty hump of green-black sea
With its womanly lip of brilliant foam

To consummate the ego-death then breach.

Come to Me

Brighter
By rain than eyes
By laughter,

A patch of lambent
Breeze fizzes with zest as where
The whale will breach.

All is Well

I choose again
To hear my silent voice

Sharing with me my knowledge
That all is well:

Like a stroked dog
I know that this is true

And see the boulder of rain
Beside the sun.

The Pursuit of Happiness

The corgi that chases the van
Wouldn't know what to do with it
Were he to catch it.

Composedly, serendipitously,
I amble along my life
Holding my hand out. Today

Magpie-shit landed in my palm
And later a painted lady
Alit briefly on my little finger!

Cranial Osteopathy
For Adrian

At seventy
A very young baby

I lie on your table
And smile my first smile

Because I hope
To make friends with Death

And so die laughing.

The Almond Tree Shall Flourish

A Gloss on *Ecclesiastes*, XII

When I came home from my walk
There you were on the bed
Flat on your back, peacefully dozing
In a white cotton top
And slightly ballooning black trousers.

Our two tabbies luxuriated
Between your outstretched legs. You looked
Composed and decorative
With your calm face and cyclamen toenails,
As in some harem à la Matisse.

I took your picture, love . . .
Then took it again. We are sixty-nine.
The grasshopper is indeed a burden
But those that look out of the windows
Are not yet darkened.

Note

This sequence, written over a period of about thirty years, has a narrative implication: it engages with a slow awakening, a journey from alcohol-dependency into sobriety. Jung coined for such a process the witty Latin motto *spiritus contra spiritum* – 'spirit [as in spirituality] against spirit [as in liquor]'.

In the poem 'Fresh Start', the words 'my own face aged two' and 'that cheerfulness' refer to a photograph of me at that age – an image that recurs in 'The Beloved' as the two-year-old sitting in a rock-pool.

With reference to the poem 'Spiritus', the meanings of the word *spiritus* in classical (as opposed to later) Latin include spirit, air and the breath of life – and not alcohol.

A few individual poems, or earlier versions of them, have appeared in *Acumen, Agenda, The Rialto, Scintilla, Stand* and *www.wanderingdog.co.uk*. Additionally, two of the poems in Part One were included in a collection published by Anvil Press in 1980 and four of them in a booklet published by the Many Press in 1991. My thanks to all concerned. Thanks too to Sophie Lewis for advice and help in preparation of the manuscript.

The epigraph to this book is taken from Volume 2 of the *Collected Letters (1951–1961)* of Carl Gustav Jung (pp. 624–5), Princeton University Press, 1976. Thanks are due to Marget Aldrich of the Press for granting permission to cite their copyright letter.

W. G. S.